A Pocket Book of Prompts

A Pocket Book of Prompts

LEAF SELIGMAN

BAUHAN PUBLISHING
PETERBOROUGH · NEW HAMPSHIRE
2015

© 2015 Leaf Seligman
All Rights Reserved

Library of Congress Cataloging-in-Publication Data

Seligman, Leaf, 1958-
A pocket book of prompts / Leaf Seligman.
     pages cm
Includes bibliographical references and index.
ISBN 978-0-87233-200-3 (alk. paper)
1. Authorship. 2. Creative writing. 3. Prompting
(Education) I. Title.
PN145.S43 2015
808.02--dc23

                              2015018861

Book design by Kirsty Anderson
Typeset in Quadraat
Cover design by Henry James
Cover image: Collage by Leaf Seligman
Manufactured by Versa Press
Author photo by Brianna Morrissey
(www.blmphoto.com)

To contact Leaf, please visit:
www.leafseligman.net or www.writing thatmatters.net

BAUHAN
PUBLISHING LLC

PO BOX 117 PETERBOROUGH NEW HAMPSHIRE 03458
                    603-567-4430
WWW.BAUHANPUBLISHING.COM

        MANUFACTURED IN THE UNITED STATES

For Kimberly Cloutier Green
and Karen Kelley

whose abiding friendship
is the greatest prompt of all.

Foreword

Whenever we write, there are two subjects: the one that initiates the writing, and the one that we discover as we follow the words. The poet Richard Hugo called these the "triggering" subjects and the "generated" subjects, and he said that one mistake writers make is to think they have some obligation to stay on topic. The "real" subject of a poem lurks somewhere in the distance, and the best way to find it is to trust that the words will lead you there. Hugo's advice startled me when I first encountered it years ago. School writing taught me that "getting off topic" was a bad idea, and I had little experience with following my own writing: on the contrary, I was used to muscling words into compliance with what I thought I wanted to say.

If I had encountered the Pocket Book of Prompts back then I would have read its white spaces as a challenge rather than an invitation. I would have wondered how it could be possible that I could think of what to say on so many topics, no matter how provocative or interesting they seemed. I would have been at a loss for words. Coincidentally, I met Leaf Seligman at about the time I began to understand writing differently. She was a fiction writer and poet, while I was a working on creative nonfiction, trying to write a book on lobsters. Since then, I've come to understand that the real challenge of writing is less in the head than in the heart. Writing is emotional work. It begins with learning to tame the impulse to see first thoughts as deficient, a response that often sours into self-criticism: the writing is not very good = I am not very good. This will not do, of course, because it will stop you from writing at all. It will also leave you with nothing to work with.

It is important to write with pleasure, which, strangely enough, is not what I learned in school. I think I found pleasure, finally, by not seeing all writing as a performance to prove how smart I am. Instead of muscling language around, I learned to hungrily follow my writing, hoping to discover what I didn't know I knew. And often enough, I did. This happened not only because I learned to lower my standards to get the work done but because I also finally understood Richard Hugo's advice about missing the target: Use the triggering subject to find the "real" one, the subject that probably couldn't be discovered any other way. This is a book rich in triggering subjects, doorways that lead to hallways with other doors that you will unlock with words you didn't expect to write. The prompts are the threshold, and the white spaces uncharted, beckoning. As you write, look back briefly and you will see Leaf quietly closing the door behind you, preparing to open another on the next page. No need to hurry there, though, because right now there are your own words pulling you along to who knows where.

—Bruce Ballenger
June, 2015

Dr. Bruce Ballenger is Professor of English at Boise State University. He is author of the best-selling textbooks *The Curious Writer*, *The Curious Researcher*, and *Crafting Truth: Short Studies in Creative Nonfiction*.

Introduction

Why a book of prompts? For all the years I've taught writing, and used writing as a way to deepen connection, to make meaning or clarify it—and even as a child writing fiction to make sense of what often felt incomprehensible—prompts have initiated the process. Sometimes they have been deliberate and imposed; other times, the universe sends them unbidden. Really, prompts surround us; we inhale them, and often sob or sweat them out, but fail to notice as we do.

The most effective prompts I've met are open-ended invitations to plumb, to re-see, or to look, listen, and engage for the first time. Unlike other artistic media, words come from within—and they often need a bit of coaxing to come out.

I've used these prompts in a variety of settings: college classrooms, prisons, congregations, programs at local hospitals, writing retreats, and one-to-one sessions. Some elicit a line or two and others lead to pages. Though I use them to encourage writing, they could just as easily become invitations to meditate, dance, sing, paint, or sculpt. Sometimes, college students will declare, "These questions are *heavy*." Although some list towards whimsy, all of them attempt to open a window to what matters.

In the first section of this book, I offer one- or two-part questions that allow the taciturn to answer in a line or two while allowing the more ambitious to wax on.

In the second section, I offer more layered queries intended to plumb deeper places that invite fuller written exploration.

In order for any of these prompts to blossom, you need to send your internal critic or editor out for coffee while you write. Think of these prompts like hugs—meant to be experienced, shared, savored, not critiqued, belittled, or compared.

As Virginia Woolf wrote in *A Room of One's Own*, "So long as you write what you wish to write, that is all that matters; and whether it matters for ages or only for hours, nobody can say." Whether we consider ourselves practiced or professional writers, students writing under duress, keepers of a journal, occasional lifters of a pen, or tappers of a keyboard, it's worth asking as we write, "What's at stake?" If nothing is, why bother?

The aim of this little volume is to elicit engagement. The earth offers us love letters every moment. Why not reply? I often tell students, "Make everything you write a love letter to the world." Some missives keen, others exult. Some ponder, grapple, even curse the pain life contains—yet as long as our words express what matters, ultimately every act of writing matters, too.

All you need is a pen. You can write here.

First Day Prompts

Often, as a way to break the ice on the first day of a college writing class, I pass around a tiny box of prompts written on strips of paper and ask each student to pull one out and respond. Over the years, students have added their own prompts, so here is a collection of accumulated, student-tested invitations to move beyond hometowns, high schools, or intended majors in search of the authentic self.

If you could change one thing about the world, what would it be?

Why?

How would you like the change to happen?

What is the most helpful thing you've done for someone else?

What motivated you to do it?

If you could go back in time, to what year/ decade/era would you go?

Where would you go?

What would you do?

What intrigues you about that time?

Have you ever accomplished a big goal?

If so, what was it?

If not, what is one you have for the future?

Name an experience (good or bad) that has changed your life and describe how.

What is one significant flaw you have?

If you could change it, would you want to?

Has someone ever made you realize that you have been behaving poorly even if you didn't realize it yourself?

If you weren't in school or didn't have to work, what would you do all day?

Does fear motivate you?

If so, what does it motivate you to do?

Does it limit you?

If so, how?

What's the best feeling you've ever had?

What occasioned it?

What comforts you?

When have you felt the most lost in life?

Describe it using all your senses.

Then describe the experience of finding yourself or of being found.

If you consider all the teachers you've had, not just in school but in life, who has taught you the most and why?

If someone were to thank you for imparting a valuable lesson, what would you want the lesson to be?

If you could choose the very last things you would see, hear, feel, taste, and smell before you die, what would they be and why?

What's the zaniest thing you've done?

Have you ever done something you told
yourself you would never do?

If so, what did you do?

Why?

If you could paint the ideal picture for where you want to be right now, what would it look like?

Use your senses, and describe the circumstances, too.

What in your life contributed most to who you are today?

If you could interview one person from history, who would it be?

Why that person?

What would you ask?

Are your nighttime dreams ever helpful?

If so, how?

What and where is your favorite place?

Describe it using all your senses.

What makes it your favorite?

If you could change an event in your life,
what would it be?

How would you change it?

Has your environment shaped your identity?

If so, how?

Is violence ever necessary?

If so, under what circumstances?

What is the most fun you've ever had?

If fun were a color, what would it be?

If it made a sound, what would it be?

What is the flavor of fun?

Its scent?

Its texture?

What makes life real to you?

If you were to inhabit a gender identity other than the one you inhabit now, what's one experience you'd like to have?

If you could choose to be born into a different culture, geography, status, nationality, religious background, or other identity, what would you choose and why?

Would you die for anyone?

If so, who?

Would you prefer a nomadic life to a settled existence?

Why or why not?

What is the scariest thing that has ever happened to you?

Describe it.

If you could be any animal for a day or a
night, what would you be?

Imagine yourself as that animal and describe
a moment using all your senses.

When have you felt engaged in your education?

When have you not?

If you could design the ideal learning environment, what would it be?

Describe five key elements.

Prompts for Deeper Reflection

Here are multifacted queries to prompt introspection and contemplation. Any of them will provide raw material that can be crafted, revised, and chiseled into art. Yet even without polishing, gems emerge, for each stone turned yields its own beauty.

What are the stories you retell?

Are they family stories, sacred stories, urban legend, personal narrative?

Do they shape your identity in any way?

Does your understanding of identity shape the way you tell the stories?

Write your autobiography in five lines.

1.

2.

3.

4.

5.

Notice what you included and what you left out. Now write a second version that does not elaborate on the first, but uses what you left out. For example, if you stated place and date of birth, family of origin, school attendance, marital or relationship status, try a version that captures the interior landscape: emotions, senses, spiritual or existential journey or transformation.

1.

2.

3.

4.

5.

Review both versions of your five-line autobiography. Reflect on the value of constraint: What does the limitation of five lines free you to leave out or compel you to include? Consider how limitation/constraint can be liberating in other aspects of life. Write about that next.

Write a five-line not-autobiography. You can invent a life for yourself in five lines or document what did not bless or befall you. What you may have escaped or missed (so far). The identities you do not inhabit. See where your invented story leads. Often, what is not our story reveals more about us and who we are than we might imagine.

1.

2.

3.

4.

5.

Zora Neale Hurston wrote, "There are years that ask questions and years that answer."

Which year are you in?

What questions does this year pose?

What answers does it provide?

If you review the past decade, what conversation emerges across the years?

Imagine that in ten minutes you would lose all your memories with the exception of what you write down now. What memories would you keep? Set a timer and start writing now.

When you finish, read what you wrote. Does anything you included or left out surprise you?

"Our job is to stay in our joy."

A friend told me she arrived at this realization during a second bout of cancer. The phrase asks implicitly about what constitutes our joy, and how we manage to inhabit it in the midst of pain, challenge, even suffering. What's your response? How's your "work ethic?"

Failure.
List the first five words that come to mind.

1.

2.

3.

4.

5.

Next, list how failure
tastes:

smells:

appears:

sounds:

feels to the touch:

If failure were weather, what kind would it be?

If failure were a mode of transportation, what would it be?

Try turning the words on this page into a poem.

What failure has instructed you most?

What are you proudest of attempting though you did not succeed? Create a metaphor for the attempt. Imagine a still image that could capture the feelings associated with it. Describe the image.

What's the story your life longs to tell?
What prevents you from telling it?
Write a dialogue between the energy of the
story awaiting release and your resistance or
hesitance to tell it. What would it take to tell
the story? Try to negotiate so that you can.
Then write it.

What's the most courageous story you could tell? The most dangerous? The most liberating? Write a flash version of each. Then celebrate your daring.

Consider disappointment. Usually we experience it when our expectations or desires go unmet. Thus, disappointment evinces a prior experience when our expectations or desires *were* met. How might disappointment occasion resilience?

And which is worse: being disappointed or disappointing another?

What might you write to your disappointed or disappointing self?

What are your essential qualities? For each one, recall an experience that embodies/manifests it and write about it using *telling* detail (something specific and revealing) so that an observer would know you possess that quality without you saying so.

Then consider your daily life. Does it invite you to express those essential qualities or demand that you mute them?

Write a credo—a list of core values you give your heart to, the values that enliven and embolden you. Now write what actions (large and/or small) you can take to bring your life into greater alignment with your core values.

Here's a variation on the previous prompt:

What matters most?

What connects you?

What disconnects you?

A wise friend once told me, "We travel in all the light we have." Sometimes we don't have enough light so we stumble or even careen into each other. Write about a time you lacked sufficient light. How does framing the experience this way change your relationship to it?

Now write about a situation when someone else careened into you. What could have offered illumination in that moment? How does reflecting through this lens affect your understanding?

If a Martian were to follow you around for a day, would the Martian be able to tell the sources of your joy?

Who and what you love?

What matters?

If so, how?

What evidence would the Martian observe to indicate what enlivens you?

When disruption summons you to the present moment, what does the summons say?

Consider a current or recent disruption. Describe it as a source of consternation or pain. Then describe it as a useful, perhaps necessary alarm.

Contemplate the concept of *holy disruption*. How can disruption deepen your connection to what is sacred or most meaningful to you?

If you could appear on YouTube or on any global news channel for ten minutes, what message would you convey and how would you convey it?

And how did you decide on your message?

For what do you wish to be remembered?

Now consider how what you wrote reflects your sense of purpose, connectedness (to whom and what you belong), and your essential nature.

If grief is a water table that rises and falls, is the ground dry, squishy or saturated today?

Consider how the source of our power or strength can also be a source of disintegration or vulnerability. Write about the source from both perspectives. For instance, how might compassion both enliven and entrap?

How might detachment allow necessary focus in the operating room yet wreak havoc at home?

Rumi, the thirteenth-century Sufi poet, asks why we stay in our prison cell when the door is open. Consider his question. What constitutes your cell?

Describe its dimensions.

What keeps you there?

Imagine leaving. Write that departure.

If you held a banquet of forgiveness, whom would you invite?

Is there anyone you worry would show up unannounced?

Is there someone else's banquet you hope to be invited to?

Carl Jung articulated the idea of our shadow side—the parts of self beyond conscious awareness or the good graces of ego. Even though a shadow can obscure light, it can only exist in the presence of light.

Consider the moon: No matter how it appears to the eye (full, crescent, or somewhere in between), its actual shape remains the same. It's always a full sphere. Think of yourself in your entirety—a physical, emotional, intellectual, spiritual being. At the same time, only a portion of who you are is visible. What goes unseen? How does the unseen portion affect your perception of self? How does it affect others' perception of you? When do you feel your fullness fully revealed? When does your fullness appear diminished?

The earth composts. Wastes nothing. What in your life could you compost?

How might it flower?

Jot down four elements or circumstances of your life that might transform were you to reimagine them as compost, not garbage. Then acquaint yourself with a living flower or plant. Notice its details and try incorporating those details into an image (a paragraph or stanza) that shows your life blooming in unforeseen ways.

What does it mean to you to live with intention?

What in your daily life feels intentional and what does not?

If you sort the intentional and non-intentional into piles, which one is larger? What does that tell you?

Who and what will you advocate for when it is not convenient?

What compels you to travel beyond your comfort zone?

Imagine a scenario where you do so. Describe it in detail. Pay attention to your senses. Notice what you notice. Try to capture a moment in words as compelling as a photograph that might make you go to your computer to learn more, send a donation, post to Facebook, or volunteer.

If you consciously practice wellness, what are the elements of your practice?

Try writing an ode to the elements and to the wellness you experience as a result.

If you do not practice wellness, what might such a practice involve?

Try composing a letter that invites the practice into your life or inspires you to undertake it.

What would it mean for you to choose
without regret? To discern so that each
choice, though it might involve risk,
hardship, even heartbreak, is one you would
make without wishing you had not?

What keeps you from choosing without
regret?
What emboldens you to do so?

If you were to paint a choice that carries
regret, what colors would you use? If you
were to give it an aroma, what would it be?
What texture? Is it lace? Burlap? The bark of
a tree? Blistered skin? What sound would it
make?

If you were to write a letter to the self that
made a choice tinged with regret, what
would you say now to that former version of
self to counsel, encourage, or console?

What does it mean to you to love wantonly, recklessly, as some wise souls suggest? Are there ways you try to love neatly, as with measuring spoons? What would it feel like to love without trying to properly apportion the love or express it perfectly?

Come up with your own metaphor. Letting a dog with muddy feet romp in your living room? Jiggling snow-flocked pine boughs to free them of their burden?

What lesson or lessons did life teach you today? In what guise did the instructor appear?

If you could learn anything today, what would it be?

If your friends were musical instruments, describe the band or orchestra they would create if you assembled them.

If you were a musical instrument what would you be? Try writing a poem (in verse or prose) expressing that experience.

What challenge do you face right now?

Does it remind you of other challenges?

Is it harder or worse than others?

What stores of strength, resilience, courage, or determination will you call upon to meet it?

Conjure an image for both your challenge and your resilience. Describe in rich sensory detail. Then choose three words from each description and craft a six-word memoir of the challenge.

My wise friend told me, "It is only in an un-condemned state that any of us can change." Believing transformation can occur makes it possible for it to occur.

Consider your life or anyone else's. How might the grace of a second or third chance re-form it?

If we never say never, what can unfold?

What constitutes your circle or circles of kinship? To whom do you belong? In what do you abide?

Explore what family, community, nature, and connection mean. Each inhalation comes from the exhalation of trees.

Breathing is a French kiss with the forest. How does that figure into your family tree?

In school, at work, and in relationships, we often feel pressured to get it right, to be sure, to be unequivocal, but certainty has its downsides.

What are they?

Jot down as many as you can. Then explore two or three in depth and write an ode or a make-up letter to uncertainty.

The rabbis translate *dayenu* as "It would have been sufficient." I translate it as "abundantly enough."

Each year at the Passover Seder, there's a litany of gratitude expressed by listing a sufficiency of blessings received.

Write your own litany.

Capture in words what it is in your life that forms an abundance of enough.

If someone were to find this *Pocket Book of Prompts* and read what you've written thus far, would the person know what matters to you?

What constitutes your essence?

Who and what and how you love?

What bugs you?

What excites you?

What makes you laugh—or cry—or fall silent?

If not, what do you need to write for that to happen?

Notes

Notes

Notes

Notes

Notes

LEAF SELIGMAN has written fervently since childhood—stories, letters to the editor, journals, poems, plays, novels, essays, sabbath meditations—and has come to understand what needs to be written and to be read. She says, "Writing has always been the primary way I make sense of my surroundings, sort out emotions, develop ideas, and connect with people." She holds a master's degree in writing from the University of New Hampshire and a master's degree in divinity from Harvard University. She has been teaching writing since 1985 at universities, colleges, prisons, jails, and in a variety of community settings. After ten years as a Unitarian Universalist minister, she is now happily living a writing-centered life in the woods of southwestern New Hampshire with her love dog, Zuki.